Our Little Lives

A Book of Poetry & Prose

Kaytlin Shehata

Second Edition published by 2021

Second Edition

To Jason,

Without your support, I would have never been able to relive these moments to write this book.

PART ONE: THE BROKEN

I'm Fine

I've been drowning for years,
Silently screaming in complete agony.
The instinct to open my mouth,
To let the ocean wash out my lungs
Is almost impossible to resist.
But once I do,
Once I let the water finish
Consuming me,
The bombs in my head will finally
cease.
They will finally come to an end.
* * *
But it's okay... I'm fine.

Little White Lies

Big white smiles,
Red wine.

Stay up all night,
Future talk.

Hold me in your sleep,
Sweet dreams.

Sun Rises,
Goodbye.

Little white lies,
Red-rimmed eyes.

Mother

When I became a mother,
I gave up my immense amount of
freedom,
My privacy, and long showers.
I gave up warm food and the
Flawlessness I once felt about my skin.
I gave up quiet time and sleeping alone.

When I became a single mother,
I gave up the image of the family I
always
dreamed of.
I gave up early Christmas mornings with
two full cups of coffee,
Sitting on the couch watching our little
ones' face light up.
I gave up shared memories of the first
steps and the first day of school.
I gave up giving my son the family I
always

thought I would have.
But most of all,
I gave up watching my little boy grow
up,
With the person, I once thought I would
Love forever.

Oblivion

Little Stones create
Black cracks
That spread across
My silk-white
Porcelain frame.
Damaged but not yet
Broken.

Little stones will eventually
Break me,
They will make my skin crumble
Before I come down,
Shattering into oblivion.

Shadow

You make me want to
Bury my
Soul
So far into the dark,
That even my
Shadow
Wouldn't be able to find it.

Tsunami

I obliterate everything in my path.
I am a cause with no good effect.
I create problems on end,
I can't even keep a friend.

I want to scream.
I want to cry.
I want to play the victim
In the novel that *I'm* writing.
I just want it all to stop.

I am a tsunami,
I obliterate the world around me.

Waves

My chest used to
Flood with
Love
When I looked at you.

Now your waves
Drown me
With every
Suffocating stare.

The Wave You Embraced

Love is like a wave,
It will build and build
Getting more robust and faster,
Becoming something so beautiful.

But then it crashes.
Out of nowhere.
You never saw your wave reach its tip,
You never saw your wave begin to curl
at its edges
And begin to roar a little louder.
You didn't hear the others telling you to
slow down,
To get out of the water.

Then you crash.
Your wave curls
Into a beautiful yet horrific cave,
That will inevitably fold in on itself.
You go from a vibrant blue

To a white foam that coats the shore.

Your wave is no more.

3 AM

The wind doesn't stir at 3 am.
It doesn't throw branches at your already
cracked windows
Or try to scream at you over your thoughts.

No.
The gusts will come in the middle of the day.
It will pull you,
Push you.
It will take your blue skies
And turn them dark.

The pain of it will hit you on your good days.
The day when you're walking through the park,
With the sun warm on your smiling face,

But there is no hand to hold, no laughter to share.

It will break you on the great days.
The days when you've just had the best news,
But you have no arms to run into.

And it will kill you on the amazing days.
The day you watch your son take his first steps,
But there is no one to look over at, no one to cheer with.
No one to share a single look to say,
"I love you."

Dear you,

I loved you. Back when I said I did, I meant it. I really did want to grow old with you. I really did plan our wedding, I had every fucking detail planned out in my head, and when you asked me to marry you, I said yes, and I fucking meant it.

But that was then.

You hit me, and I forgave you because I was stupid and in love and there were just so many fucking complications to leaving you. And I thought I needed you. But I didn't. And I don't. And fuck, I'm sick of writing about you.

I've cleaned you from my life. Your side of the bed has been slept on. Your scent no longer lingers in this place. I have had my last nightmare of you. I am finally free from your grasp and I'm a fucking bird, no I'm a mother fucking eagle, and I'm soaring without you.

Fuck you.

Goodbye,

Me.

"I thought I killed you,"
Followed by tear-soaked eyes.
Turned into,
"I could have killed you,"
From a rage-filled heart.

Water slips over the edges of the tub, almost invisible. It would be impossible to tell but the floor gets soaked every time I move a part of my body. Just a slight wiggle of a finger was all it took to send the water cascading down to the tiles.

The music in the background was soft, nothing loud, but nothing too quiet either. Its sounds trickle through each ear, words blistering my brain.

My eyes drift up, the ceiling, almost seamless, except for a small crack floating away from the corner. A million imperfections waiting to break free. I close my eyes, take one long breath, and submerge myself.

Peace.

Muffled sounds are floating in and out of my brain. The water, tumbling to the floor with a softer splash. The music, beating along with my pulse. I invite the water to sting my eyes, and I'm there again, looking at the ceiling, but this time it's full of imperfections, they move with the waves created by my body losing itself.

The world above me keeps spinning, it waits for no one, and it lives its own life. It breathes through the pain, the hurt, and the sadness. It fights through, it creates its own joy. It gives us gifts and takes them away. Will it take me away? Do I have that kind of choice? Do I make my own fate? Or is it already written out? Will every single decision lead to the same end?

I want to be like the world, I want to soar, to live, to love, to breathe. I want to push myself to the brink of death and come back fighting. I want to prove that I am not just another body walking down the streets. I am not just another face on a screen. I am bigger and prouder and louder than that.

I am me.

My lungs begin to ache and the water around me begins to swirl, sounds from the outside world are entering the tub. I can hear the cars buzzing past my window, the people talking, laughing, crying, and screaming. Emotions slice through every inch of me. I want to feel it, I want to feel it all. Give it to me, World. I'm waiting. Hit me with everything you got, 'cause I'm not leaving. Not yet.

My body rips from the grip of the bottom of the tub, and I come breaking through the barrier that divides me from the world.

More water spills from the tub. I stare at the mess I've created.

Fuck, I'm gonna need more towels.

FU

The ocean took me in,
Soft, smooth, and beautiful.
It told me it loved me,
It pretended to soothe me with
its waves.
It manipulated me in ways
I didn't know possible.

But when I started to see it,
When I started to fight it,
The current just became more vigorous,
More aggressive.
Its waves became ten-foot monsters
That tried to drown me,
Its hands gripped my throat,
And its fists smashed into me.

I tried to swim,
I tried to fight it,
I tried to be strong.

But it had enough,
It lifted me up in the biggest wave
it could conjure,
I was at the top and the fear was never
so immense,
It lifted me up and threw me to the
shore,
Where I landed on nothing but my neck.

Data

I try to be concrete.
I try to base decisions on facts and data.
The things I can touch, not feel.
This way, life might be a little less
painful,
If I let statistics choose.

But,

Sometimes, I yearn for a love
That tears my soul in two.
Sometimes, I crave the idea
Of letting loose,
Of letting fate decide.
Sometimes, I want to live for life,
Believe in it.

Sometimes, I want to let myself
love you.
But if I do,

I may not be able to survive
If I lost you

Find Me

I look in the mirror and search for the girl I used to be.
The one whose eyes lit up at the sound of the morning.
The one whose love reached every corner of the Earth.
The one whose smile was bright and true.

I look in the mirror and search for that girl,
And find her hiding in the shadows of my face.
She's there,
She's always been there.
She's just been too afraid to shine the way she used to.

I reach down into myself and try to pull her out.

I need her,
I need her smile,
Her laugh,
Her happiness.
I need the sun to shine in my
heart again.

Stay Away

I heard you on the radio today.
It was like a wave from the past
Smashed into my car
And came blaring through the speakers.

My heart began to ache
In a way, I thought
It would never ache again.
In a way, it only hurt when
I was with you.

I tried to ignore the memories
The flashes of your face in my mind.
I'm happy now.
I used this thought to try and pry you
From my brain,
But you're more stubborn
Then you used to be.
At this moment, you don't want to leave
You want to feast on my discomfort.

Your voice fades from the radio.

But you stay content in my brain.

Glass

I am a bird in a room made of glass.
I can see the world.
I can see all the other birds,
Playing and laughing.
I can see the blue skies
And the green trees.
But anytime I think there's a weak spot,
I go crashing into the glass,
Breaking a wing.

I am a bird in a room made of glass,
Mangled and barely breathing

Ocean Abyss

Your love is like an ocean
That spins me into an enormous abyss.
The waves forming currents,
Strong enough to pull an elephant
Into the whirlpool of hunger,
The monsters swimming beneath me
Tumble into one another,
The strong feeding off the weak.

I gasp for air,
My arms and legs moving,
Splashing,
At an impossible rate.
Millions of thoughts tumble
Through my brain,
Cascading out of me
Without a single filter,
Without a single regret.

Your Wave Killed Me

There was a time when your arms
wrapped
around me, and all I felt was warmth.
There was a time when a single look was
all
I needed to know exactly what you were
thinking.
There was a time when you said
"I love you,"
and I believed it.

Now, when you get close to me, I flinch
Now, when you look at me I see the eyes
of a stranger.
Now, when you say "I love you," I don't
believe a single word.

We once moved together, like a wave in
the ocean.
Smooth, soft, beautiful.

We were a gorgeous blue that sang
with the wind.
However, one night,
The clouds rolled in,
The wind screamed at us,
The storm tore at our seams.
It battered me,
It warped you,
It broke us.

Our wave slammed against the shore,
Shattering us into a million pieces.
Little parts of each of us
Disappeared into the sand,

Gone forever.

As the ocean pulled us back in,
We were disembodied from each other,
Our fingers no longer touched,
My eyes never looked into yours again,
The only feeling that ever coursed
through me
Was fear.

The love in your heart ran away,
Even that was scared of you.

She loved him.
Not in butterflies in the stomach kind of way.
She loved him because of his faults.
She loved him because when he got sick, he would cuddle up next to her and sniffle in her ear.
She loved him because when she would watch TV he wouldn't stop talking and she could never hear what was going on. She loved him because when she would cry, he would make her laugh.
She loved him for everything he had in him.
Both good and bad.

He had a lust for her.
He wanted one thing and he didn't care how he got it.

Manipulative words rolled off his
tongue,
He convinced her that he was in love,
He told her that he wanted her forever.
He lied.

She was scared of him.
Time went by, she started to see the
lies.
She started to see the anger.
She noticed that sex was more
important
than her feelings.
She hid.

He was angry.
He could feel her pulling away, his
temper
rose.
The fighting got worse.

She loved him, she told herself.
She let him carry on.

He didn't stop.
Words became fists,
Threats became broken memories
scattered
on the floor.

He broke her.

She hated him.

PART TWO: THE LOVERS

Before I Touched Your Skin

I fell in love with you before I touched your skin.
It was your crooked smile with a dimple playing peek-a-boo,
And those beautiful blues that I can never seem to stop looking in.
I fell for that laugh, and the way your voice rang in my ears.
For that passion in your tone, and the way that you move.
You weren't hard to fall for.
I just hope you're a good catcher.

My Promise To You

There was an ocean in my lungs
Silently drowning me from the inside.
The waves plunged through me
The coral ripped me to pieces
The sand choked me.

But then you saved me,
You breathed your air into me.
You took my battered body
And filled me up.

And now I stand here
Before you.
I stand here and promise
To have, to hold.
For better, or worse.

I promise, to love
To laugh, to live

I stand here before you,
And choose to love you
Every day.
Forever.

Love Might Be

Just picture it.
Ten years from now,
A loveseat and a piano.
A bottle of wine and a good book,
The kids dancing to the music.
And you playing the most beautiful song
I have ever heard.

I can see it in your eyes,
In the way, we move as one.

You have taught me that maybe,
Just maybe.

Love could be real.

Thank you.

You

You saved me, ya know.
From the day I let you embrace my slouched shoulders.
You lifted me up and taught me composure.
You brought me from the shadows of my soul, proving to me that I could be bright,
happy, and alive further than in my own head.

Thank you, thank you for teaching me a little more about myself.

Thank you for bringing out the pieces I thought I once lost forever.

Home

Let me be your ocean.

Let me be the waves
That soothes you in a storm.
Enable me to be the vast openness
That keeps your breathing steady.
I want to be the wind,
That carries your screams away.

Let me be your escape.

I want to be the one you run to
When the rest of the world shuts
the door.
Show me that it's okay
To hold you when you can't stay
standing.
Let me be your flashlight
When the darkness gets too thick.

Let me be your home.

Tornado

You are a tornado.
You burrow through me,
You suck the wind out of me,
You wrap me up as if I was nothing,
But your own.

Love Is

He didn't love me.
He loved the way I made him feel
About himself.

That's not love.

Love is,
Loving someone for them,
Not wanting or needing anything from them.

Love is,
Looking at her sleeping next to you,
And feeling like you're soaring
Because she is, and will always be,
The most breathtaking sight.

Love is,
Laughs, and inside jokes.

It's crying in the arms of someone who will never let go,
And being that person for them when they need it.

Love is,
2 am fights,
That can be made up with a hug.

Love is,
Looking your best friend in the eyes,
And promising forever.

Love is not selfish.
Love is giving, and taking, and forever.

PART THREE: THE SELF DISCOVERERS

Believe

I choose to believe.

I choose to believe in the world and the people that roam it.
I choose to love and to care for my enemies,
The ones who live inside of me,
And the ones who walk around me.
I choose to move past all the bad things that have happened,
To use them as lessons, not restrictions.

I choose to believe that people will learn from the mistakes they make.

Maybe that makes me naïve,
But I don't really care.

Monsters

At the age of ten
The monsters under my bed
Were easily whisked away by my
parents.
All they had to do was come in and check
To see if my fear and paranoia
Was strong enough to create such a
Monstrous being.

At the age of twenty
The monsters lurking in the corner,
Hiding in the closet,
And waiting under the bed
Are versions of myself.
They are my mistakes my demons,
My faults.
They are my false words, my anger,
My wrongs.

My mind finally created

These monstrous beings.
The ones who come out when
The sun goes down,
The lights go off,
And all that's left are
My thoughts and I.

Ocean

If the ocean were my friend,
It wouldn't engulf me the way it does.
Its deep whispers wouldn't pull me
Into absence
Its alluring tide wouldn't
Wash me into oblivion.

* * *

Occasionally though,
I embrace it.
I enjoy the feeling of the water
Washing out my lungs
Hoping that one day
I will be clean again.

You were like skydiving,
Free falling through the sky.
I hated you.
I loved you.
And I was absolutely terrified,
Of never being caught.
* * *
You didn't catch me,
But that's fine.

I caught myself.

Today

I'm grateful for the hurt.
For the broken hearts and
misunderstandings.
For the wrong left turns and the river
of tears.
I'm grateful for the homelessness,
The abuse,
And the little pieces of myself
That was stolen.

I'm thankful that I am now
Strong,
Ambitious,
And alive.

I'm thankful for all the
Pain
You caused me.

Because without it,

I would never be
The woman I am today.

In The Ground

You, can't live your life
Staring at the ground.

Because one day,
You're going to end up in it
And realize,
You never knew what
The sky looked like.

Balloon

I am a balloon fastened to nothing.
Floating above the world,
Seeing it at a distance.

People, millions of people.
Like stars in the sky,
Blinking in and out of existence
As the clouds roll by.
Their complex voices creep through me,
Their muffles words
Silence me into inanimateness.

I want to break free
From this hold on nothing.
I want to be tethered
To something
To anything.
Please,
Take me in.
Hold me,

Love me,
Choose me.

I am a balloon.
Floating away.

Nonexistent.

Seeing Her

She stares at the stranger in the mirror,
The one she's been looking at for years.
The one whose eyes she cannot
recognize.
The one whose smile is made from
cosmetics.
The one whose silence is more violent,
Then a tsunami at its peak.

She stares...
And for the first time, she can *see* her.

She can see the longing in her eyes.
The want, the need. For something,
someone
To save her.

She can see the disappointment
Behind the makeup.
The hate she feels for herself.

Kicking her back down the second
She even looks towards the sky.

She can hear past the silence,
The screams breaking through,
The sobs rattled every inch of her body.

She looks up.
Her eyes bleeding the tears
She's been holding back for years.

She sees that, the stranger in the
mirror
Blurs together to create an image she
can finally
Recognize.

24 Hours

Happiness is not a destination,
happiness is now.
One day,
24 hours,
1,440 minutes,
86,400 seconds.

We always have one more day,
until we don't.

Life is not a guarantee,
it's a chance, a gamble.
Life is a laugh,
a cry,
a smile,
it's a song being sung
and a guitar being strung.

It's a memory,
a glance,

a vow,
a dance.

It's a million and one thoughts
buzzing through your head.

It's no umbrella on a day
where the skies have opened up.

It's the first kiss,
And a moment,
Life is now,
Happiness is always.

Dear Me

Breathe,
Laugh,
And feel the weight of
The world
Lift off your chest.

You may not know
How long you have
On the ground beneath you,
But you do have
Today.
You have now.
So love,
Be kind,
And live like you
Don't get
Tomorrow.

Home

It's not four walls and a roof
Over your head.
Not some destination on a map.

It's the feeling of
Salty wind hitting your face
And running through your hair.
It's the touch of a stranger
That electrifies your entire body.
And it's the hug of a child,
That you made from scratch.

It's your heart.

How is it that this is what I needed, this is what I need to be happy again, to find out who I really am? Yet, I feel like my heart could stop any minute now, that I am without you. Every time I look at your face I want to pull you back into my arms and tell you this will be okay. But it won't be okay. If I forgive you now, we will be back here in a month... I will be hurting, you won't be listening, and I can't learn to love myself that way.

All Alone

Headlights peer at me through my windshield. Two piercing eyes pass me by. Two by two. We fly by each other in a matter of seconds, as if neither of us was even there at all.

I watch as the stream of headlights come and go. I count, one. Two. Three. Each light attaches to a piece of steel and rubber which holds a person, a family. Someone's brother, sister, mother, father, daughter, or son. Every piece of metal passing by me holds a story, a life, a feeling. Some may sit in silence, while others in noise. Some are going towards something, and some may be going away.

People, millions of people. Millions of stories. Millions of lives go by in a flash.

Millions of lives passed me by as if each one was never there at all.

PART FOUR: STICKY NOTE QUOTES

#1

All you get is yourself,
And it would be a shame
To waste a life
Wishing
For something you
Can't have
Instead of working
Towards something
You deserve.

#2

I wouldn't call you
My muse.
But you make me
Want to go on.

#3

Telling me
Not to think about him,
Is like asking me to
Breathe underwater.

Impossible and suffocating.

#4

Love is so dangerously blinding,
You don't see the
Gun
Pointed at your head
Until the barrel is cold
Up against
Your temple.

#5

My brain shuffles
The scenes my life
Has portrayed,
Trying to find a purpose
For the day by day.

Where everything
Always stays the same.

#6

I hang on
To your every
Word,
Like driftwood
Keeping me
Afloat.

#7

Sometimes,
It's like finding out
That a scratch in a
Mirror
Is actually
Just a broken piece
Of yourself.

#8

I tried to
Write you something
New,
But all I could think
Was how much
I miss you.

#9

I'd rather feel
Nothing at all
Then the wave of
Your old love,
That crashes into me
Every time
I close
My eyes.

#10

There are
A million
Songs
On the
Radio
Trying to
Teach me
How to
Love you.

#11

You make the
Sun rise,
After all my damn days
Of cloudy skies.

#12

I cry for the
Man
You used to be.
Not the one that
Was left
When I
Walked away.

#13

I guess the
Words that flow
From my mouth
Don’t hold the
Weight I always
Thought they did.

Acknowledgments

Writing a book is rarely a solitary endeavor; it is built on the support and encouragement of many incredible individuals and communities. To all those who have touched my life and inspired these words, I extend my deepest gratitude.

First and foremost, I thank my readers – those who have bravely embarked on this journey through the pages of my thoughts and emotions. Your openness to connect with these themes of mental health, abuse, and the pursuit of love is what fuels my passion for writing.

I owe a debt of thanks to my family and my wonderful husband, whose unwavering love has been both my foundation and my strength. Your patience and understanding during moments of solitude and introspection have been invaluable.

I am grateful to the mental health professionals and advocates whose work has enlightened and inspired me. Your dedication to healing and understanding has informed the themes explored in these pages.

Lastly, to anyone who has experienced similar struggles or triumphs, your resilience has reminded me of the universality of human emotions and the power of storytelling.

This book is a testament to the courage of those who confront their innermost battles and emerge with newfound strength and clarity. May these words resonate with you as they have with me.

www.ingramcontent.com/pod-product-compliance
Lightning Source LLC
Chambersburg PA
CBHW021335160726
47994CB00007B/2711

* 9 7 9 8 8 6 9 1 8 9 2 4 0 *